Feminist Icons

Feminist Icons

of the
19th and
Early 20th Century

Colleen Glen

BInk

Bink Books

Bedazzled Ink Publishing Company • Fairfield, California

978-1-949290-46-2 paperback

Cover Design
by

Illustrations
by
C.A. Casey

Women and Books

Bink Books
a division of
Bedazzled Ink Publishing, LLC
Fairfield, California
http://www.bedazzledink.com

Note

There are many, many notable women from this time period who could be considered feminists for the things they did. Here I have listed some who were pivotal in building a world in which women had bodily autonomy, women who specifically contributed to the women's movement of the time.

When learning about history and women's roles in history, usually we see a theme of women not being able to shape their own lives. Women didn't do things, things were done to them. The mid to late nineteenth century is a remarkable period of time, because in studying this era, we can see that marriage and fertility rates were significantly lower than ever before, whereas before this time, marriage and family was the only life available to women. At this time, women were beginning to take control of their own lives and bodies, and they were helped along by some of the women listed here.

Emma Goldman

Emma Goldman was born June 27, 1869 in the city of Kovno, Russia, which is now Lithuania, into an Orthodox Jewish family. Her parents, Abraham and Taube Goldman, were shopkeepers, and Emma was the third of six children. Her childhood was not a happy one, as her father was a violent drunk and her mother distant. Her father was particularly impatient of Emma's rebellious nature, which was apparent even when she was a child.

This was a time of social reform under the rule of Alexander II. Most notably, an 1861 law freed the serfs of Russia from their dependence on their landowners. Like most places in the world at this time, there was significant industrial growth, as well as judicial, cultural, and educational reforms. Despite these reforms there was still much political unrest in Russia, and Alexander II was assassinated in 1881.

Goldman's father took her out of school when she was a teenager, planning to arrange a marriage for her when she was fifteen, but she instead emigrated to the United States with her sister in 1885. They joined their other sister in Rochester, NY and Goldman found a job as a seamstress in a factory. Like all factory work during the Industrial

Revolution, the conditions were brutal, the hours long, and the pay minimal. This is the time that the seeds of her interest in the labor movement and anarchism were planted. She started joining radical groups that were pushing for shorter work days and better working conditions.

In 1889, at the age of twenty, Goldman moved to New York City. She befriended notable anarchists there, such as Johann J. Most, publisher of *Die Freiheit*, and Alexander Berkman, who she became romantically involved with and remained close to for the rest of her life. She became a well-known anarchist in her own right, traveling, lecturing, and publishing her writings. At this point she was under investigation for her outspoken views and given the nickname Red Emma.

> "I want freedom, the right to self-expression, everybody's right to beautiful, radiant things. Anarchism meant that to me, and I would live it in spite of the whole world—prisons, persecution, everything. Yes, even in spite of the condemnation of my own closest comrades I would live my beautiful ideal."
> —Emma Goldman, *Living My Life*

She was jailed for a short time in 1893 for inciting a riot, and after her release, went to Vienna to train as a nurse and midwife, returning to New York when she was done with her studies. In 1901 she was accused of being a conspirator in the assassination of President William McKinley, because the man that shot him twice in the abdomen was a fellow anarchist who had attended one of Goldman's lectures. No charges were ever pressed, but she became infamous across the country.

Goldman published a magazine called *Mother Earth* from 1906-1917, and it became the leading voice in feminism and anarchism. She was married twice, with disastrous results, and was outspoken about her thoughts on marriage, saying it robbed women of their independence. At this time, she became romantically involved with Ben Reitman, also known as King of the Hobos. He was also a well-known activist and went on to become her manager.

When the United States became involved in World War I in 1917, Goldman joined with several other activists to form the No-Conscription League, in opposition of the draft. Goldman was arrested for these activities and charged with conspiracy to prevent draft registration. She was convicted and was sentenced to two years in prison, as well as given $10,000 in fines. In 1919 they were both deported to Russia, along with hundreds of other activists and anarchists.

Goldman was happy to move back to Russia now that the Bolshevik Revolution had toppled the Czar, but the reality of the new government soon became apparent. She said, "The old cruel regime . . . has simply been replaced by a new, equally cruel one." Goldman left Russia in 1921 and went to Germany. There she wrote *My Disillusionment in Russia* in 1923. In 1924 she moved to England and soon after married James Colton, a Scottish anarchist. This gave her the opportunity to become a British citizen, obtain a British passport, and maybe someday to be able to return to the United States, which was ultimately her goal. She spent time traveling through Europe lecturing, and in 1931 published her autobiography, *Living My Life*.

In 1934, Goldman was able to return to the United States for ninety days to travel and lecture, then returned to Europe. While visiting Canada in 1940, Goldman suffered a stroke, and she died several months later, on May 14, 1940. Her body was brought to Chicago to be buried.

Margaret Sanger

Margaret Sanger (born Higgins) was born September 14, 1879 in Corning, New York. She was one of eleven children born to Michael and Ann Higgins, a working-class Irish-Catholic couple. Later in her life, Sanger attributes her mother's many pregnancies and miscarriages to her poor health and eventual early death at the age of forty. Her father was a stonemason, but was often drinking instead of working, and the family lived in poverty.

In 1869, Sanger went on to attend Claverack College and Hudson River Institute, then went on to study nursing at White Plains Hospital. In 1902, she married an architect named William Sanger, and eventually they had three children. In 1910, the family moved to Greenwich Village in Manhattan. There they became acquainted with people such as Upton Sinclair and Emma Goldman, as well as with new and radical ways of thinking. Sanger joined the Women's Committee of the New York Socialist Party and the Liberal Club. She became involved in the labor movement and a supporter of unions and participated in several strikes.

Sanger's career in sexual education began when she had an article published called "What every girl should know." At this time, she was working as a nurse on the Lower East Side, a neighborhood that, at the time, was mostly made up of poor, underserved immigrants. She treated many women who had had back alley abortions or tried to abort their fetuses themselves and became a staunch believer in making birth control and contraceptives available for women. She is quoted saying, "No woman can call herself free until she can choose consciously whether she will or will not be a mother."

"Every child should be a wanted child."
— Margaret Sanger

In 1914, Sanger began a magazine called *The Woman Rebel*, a publication that promoted birth control. Because of the Comstock Act, which made illegal the circulation of "obscene and immoral materials" (which included anything relating to contraceptives or information about contraceptives), Sanger was forced to flee to England to avoid a possible five-year prison sentence. While there she contributed to the feminist movement and learned about many different kinds of contraceptives, including diaphragms, which she eventually smuggled back to the United States. At this point she was divorced, and she went on to have affairs with writer H.G. Wells and psychologist Havelock Ellis.

The charges against Sanger were dropped in 1915 and she was able to return to the United States, and in 1916 she opened the first birth control clinic in the U.S, actually coining the term "birth control" herself. Sanger, her sister Ethel, and the rest of the staff were arrested during a raid of their Brooklyn location only nine days after opening. They were charged with providing birth control and fitting women with diaphragms, and they sat in jail for thirty days. She appealed her conviction, and while the court wouldn't overturn its previous ruling, they made an exception in the law to allow doctors to prescribe birth control to women for medical reasons. Around this time, Sanger first started publishing *The Birth Control Review.* In

1923, she opened the Birth Control Clinical Research Bureau, which was the first legal birth control clinic in the country. Around the same time, she married her second husband, businessman J. Noah H. Slee. He provided much needed funding for her various social reform projects.

Sanger served as president of the American Birth Control League until 1928, then in 1929 started the National Committee on Federal Legislation for Birth Control. The purpose of this committee was to make it legal for doctors to distribute birth control. In 1936 it became legal to import birth control devices to the U.S., which was largely due to Sanger and her tireless efforts.

For all of the good that Sanger did for the women's movement and for women's bodily autonomy, some of her views were controversial and, by today's standards, abhorrent. Sanger was outspoken about her support for eugenics, the science of selective breeding in order to improve the human race. She felt that the mentally ill and impaired should be sterilized and that birth control could be used as a tool for eugenics. Unfortunately, these were commonly held views in the United States at the time.

Sanger stopped working for a while and moved to Tucson, Arizona, but her retirement didn't last. She traveled in Europe and Asia, working with birth control issues there, and eventually established the International Planned Parenthood Federation in 1952. She had the idea of a "magic pill" and in the early 1950s worked with a human reproduction expert named Gregory Pincus to make it a reality. An heiress named Katherine McCormick provided funding for the project, and eventually they produced the first oral contraceptive, called Envoid, which was approved by the FDA in 1960, and by 1965 married couples were legally allowed access to it.

Sanger died in a nursing home in Tucson in 1966.

Ann Trow Lohman

a.k.a. Madam Restell

Ann Trow Lohman (born Trow) was born in May of 1812 in Painswick, England. Not much is known about her parents except that her father was a laborer. She had little formal education and had to begin working as a maid at the age of fifteen. A year later she married Henry Summers, a tailor, and they had a daughter, who they named Caroline, in 1830.

In 1831, the family left England for New York City, where they settled in Lower Manhattan. Unfortunately, Henry became ill and died shortly after they arrived. Ann had to become a seamstress to support herself, taking her work home with her to watch over baby Caroline.

In 1863, she met a man named Charles Lohman, who worked as a printer at the *New York Herald*. He was literate and educated, and he could often be found at a bookstore on Chatham Street, where many of the city's radical thinkers gathered, socialized, and debated. He began to publish literature about contraception and population control. He also went on to become her husband.

Charles was pivotal in sparking Ann's medicine business, concocting a story with her of a trip to Europe where Ann trained to be a midwife with her grandmother, a French physician named

Restell. When she came back to the United States, she took on the name Mrs. Restell, later changing it to Madame Restell. She posted her first advertisement in the New York Sun on March 18, 1839.

It read:

> TO MARRIED WOMEN.—Is it not but too well known that the families of the married often increase beyond what the happiness of those who give birth to them would dictate? . . . Is it moral for parents to increase their families, regardless of consequences to themselves, or the wellbeing of their offspring, when a simple, easy, healthy, and certain remedy is within our control? The advertiser, feeling the importance of this subject, and estimating the vast benefit resulting to thousands by the adoption of means prescribed by her, has opened an office, where married females can obtain the desired information.

Women seeking treatment would go to her office on Greenwich Street, or, if they couldn't go there in person, could get treatment through the mail—Preventative Powder for five dollars per package, or Female Monthly Pills for one dollar each. These were herbal abortifacients that had been around for centuries and sometimes worked. The medications were manufactured by Ann's brother, Joseph F. Trow, who worked in a pharmacy. If these treatments did not work, the clients would come back to her office for a surgical abortion. She charged twenty dollars for the poor, a hundred dollars for the rich.

Her business flourished, and many other physicians began to take up the practice of female medicine. She warned her clients to "beware of competitors." In order to keep her business thriving, she began housing clients with unwanted pregnancies in a boarding house where they could give birth privately, and for an additional fee she would help adopt the babies out to parents who wanted them.

She began to receive letters from grateful clients numbering in the thousands.

At the time Lohman began practicing female medicine, state law reflected folk wisdom, that a fetus wasn't alive until it was "quick" or until the mother first felt it move. Abortion itself was legal, but if performed after the quickening she risked a fine or a one-year prison sentence.

Ann's first run-in with the law was in 1841, when she performed an abortion on a woman who later died. In 1846, she had another incident when a seventeen-year-old woman gave birth to a baby girl at Madame Restell's boarding house. The baby was given up for adoption, and the young woman complained to the mayor that it had been against her will. Lohman was found innocent, but the public was outraged. On February 21, an editorial was published in the *National Police Gazette* denouncing Madame Restell, and the next day a mob descended on her home. The mayor promised that he would do anything in his power to see Lohman imprisoned.

In 1847, Lohman performed an abortion upon a woman named Marie Bodine and was charged with manslaughter. Many clinical details of the abortion were made public during the trial, and public outrage grew against Madame Restell. She was convicted of a lesser charge and served a year in Blackwell's Island prison. She was treated very well there, so well, in fact, that the board of aldermen saw fit to dismiss the warden.

In 1848, the Lohmans moved their practice to a larger establishment on Chambers Street. They renovated it into a hospital and used it to distribute medicines. Then in 1864, they moved into a four-story brownstone uptown 52nd Street and 5th Avenue. The business, at this point, was mostly ignored by the law and the public. Her husband Charles died in 1878.

Later that year, Lohman had another brush with the law. Anthony Comstock, the secretary for the New York Society for the Suppression of Vice, acted as a customer and bought contraceptives from Madame Restell's establishment. Under the law that Comstock himself had created, it was illegal to possess or sell anything to do with contraceptives. He was able to come back with a search warrant to gather evidence against her.

On the morning of April 1, the date of her trial, Lohman slit her throat with a butcher knife in her bath tub. There were no funeral services held, and she was buried next to her husband in Sleepy Hollow Cemetery in Tarrytown, New York. Her estate, worth an estimated one million dollars, was awarded to her daughter and step grandchildren. After her death, her attorney stated, "Everything that the papers published she read with intense interest. She was deeply affected by all that was said against her."

Sojourner Truth

Sojourner Truth (born Isabella Bomfree) was born into slavery in Dutch-speaking Ulster County, New York the year 1797. Her parents were James and Betsy, property of Colonel Johannes Hardenbergh. She spoke only Dutch, and like the vast majority of slaves she could not read or write. She was separated from her family by the age of nine. She married around 1815 and bore five children—Diana (1815), Peter (1851), Elizabeth (1825), Sophia (1816), and another who died in infancy. Like most slaves in the North, she was isolated from other slaves, and, like slaves everywhere, was physically and sexually abused by her masters. Because of a "conversation with God" she decided to escape from her miserable existence and walk to freedom, caring her youngest, Sophia, on her back.

Bomfree settled in New York City until 1843, when she decided to travel the country as a preacher and changed her name to Sojourner Truth. She purchased a home in Northampton, Massachusetts and one in Ohio and traveled around the East and Midwest preaching for human rights. She spoke of the abolition of slavery and the emancipation of women, as well as prison reform and the termination of capital punishment. She became a powerful figurehead in these social movements, and she met many other activists like herself, such as Amy Post, Parker Pillsbury, Susan B. Anthony, Frances Dana Gage, Wendell Phillips, Laura Haviland, Lucretia Mott, and Harriet Beecher Stowe.

To support herself, Truth sold portraits that read "I sell the Shadow to support the Substance" and also received royalties from her biography, *The Narrative of Sojourner Truth, a Northern Slave*, written by her friend, Olive Gilbert in 1950. Truth's grandson, Sammy Banks, would often come with her on her lecture tours and was an invaluable asset to her, as she still could not read and write. He died at the age of twenty-four in 1875.

On May 28, 1851, Truth made one of her most famous lectures, called "Ain't I a Woman?" at a Women's Rights Convention in Akron, Ohio. She believed that women were equal in capability as men and therefor deserved the same rights as men. She said, "I have plowed and reaped and husked and chopped and mowed, and can any man do more than that? . . . And how came Jesus into the world? Through God who created him and the woman who bore him. Man, where was your part?"

Truth's sense of humor was well known. Of other women's rights activists she is quoted saying, "What kind of reformers be you, with goose-wings on your heads, as if you were going to fly, and dressed in such ridiculous fashion, talking about reform and women's rights?"

"Truth is powerful and it prevails."
— Sojourner Truth

In 1856, Truth came to Battle Creek, Michigan, where she was invited to give a lecture for a radical Quaker group, the Friends of Human Progress. The next year she settled in nearby Harmonia. She lived there for ten years before moving to Battle Creek and converted a barn on College Street into her home and lived there with her daughters, Diana and Elizabeth.

While living in Michigan she continued to fight for human rights. In the 1860s, thousands of former slaves fled to Washington D.C.

seeking a better life, but there was no employment, little food, and no suitable housing. Truth worked in Freedman's village and for the Freedman's Bureau trying to raise their standard of living. She learned of Maryland residents coming to Freedman's Village and stealing children, and she encouraged the parents to protest. The commanders of the camp told her that if she didn't stop, they would imprison her, to which she replied that, if they tried, she would "make this nation rock like a cradle." One of the methods she used to help these people was to relocate families to western states. She lobbied the government to give them land and pay for their transportation and for their new homes. She was not actively a part of the Underground Railroad, but she helped many escaped slaves and freed men and women who were.

Truth died in her home on College Street on November 26, 1883. A thousand people reportedly came to her funeral at the Congregational-Presbyterian Church. She was buried in the Oak Hill Cemetery in Battle Creek.

Lucretia
Coffin Mott

L ucretia Coffin Mott was born January 3, 1793 on Nantucket Island, Massachusetts. She was the second of the five children of Thomas Coffin Jr. and Anna Folger Mott. Her father worked as a ship's captain and was away from the family for long stretches of time, and when Lucretia was ten, he moved the family to Boston and became a merchant.

Lucretia and her family were Quakers, a religion that centers around the equality of all people under God. She attended a Quaker boarding school in upstate New York, where she later became a teacher. The family moved to Philadelphia in 1809, and she married James Mott two years later. The couple would go on to have six children together.

In 1815, Mott's father died, leaving her mother with a mountain of debt. To become financially stable again, Mott, her husband, and her mother joined forces. Mott was a teacher, her mother ran a shop, and her husband had a textile business.

In the 1830s, Mott and her husband spoke out for the abolitionist cause and joined William Lloyd Garrison's American Anti-Slavery Society. Garrison was encouraging of women to participate in the movement. Mott went on to be one of the founders of the

Philadelphia Female Anti-Slavery Society in 1933. She was a public speaker and was not deterred by people saying that she didn't behave appropriately for someone of her sex.

"The world has never yet seen a truly great and virtuous nation because in the degradation of woman the very fountains of life are poisoned at their source." — Lucretia Mott

Mott participated at the World Anti-Slavery Convention in London in 1840. There she met Elizabeth Cady Stanton. The two women were angered that they were not allowed to participate in the proceedings of the convention, and they swore that they would create a women's rights convention when they returned to the United States. This came to fruition eight years later, in 1848, when they organized the Seneca Fall Convention. Hundreds of people attended, including abolitionist Frederick Douglas. Stanton presented a "Declaration of Sentiments," demanding rights for women and the insertion of the word women into the Declaration of Independence. They also listed eighteen specific demands, including the right to divorce, property, and custody rights, and the right to vote. The latter is what sparked the women's suffrage movement. Mott is quoted saying that she was "so thoroughly imbued with women's rights that it was the most important question." Mott spoke at other conventions and published *Discourse on Women*, a detailed account of the history of women's repression. She wrote that women's limited role in society was because of limited education rather than inferiority.

Mott and her husband protested the Fugitive Slave Act of 1850 (nicknamed the Bloodhound Law by abolitionists), which stated that all escaped slaves, upon capture, be returned to their masters and that officials and citizens of free states had to cooperate. A few years later she helped an enslaved person escape bondage. In 1866, Mott became the first president of the American Equal Rights Association. She protested the fact that the fourteenth and fifteenth amendments granted the right to vote to black men but not to women.

After the Civil War, when many abolitionists thought their work was done, Mott threw herself into the cause of black suffrage. In 1864 she helped establish Swarthmore College, a coeducational institution. Two years after that, she was elected head of the American Equal Rights Association, despite her poor health. The Association later broke into two groups, the National Woman Suffrage Association (headed by Elizabeth Cady Stanton and Susan B. Anthony) and the American Woman Suffrage Association (headed by Lucy Stone, Julia Ward Howe, and others).

Mott died on November 11, 1880 in Chelton Hills (now part of Philadelphia), Pennsylvania.

Lucy Stone

Lucy Stone was born on August 13, 1818 to Francis and Hannah Stone. She was one of nine children, and the family lived in West Brookfield, Massachusetts. Her parents were both committed abolitionists.

After watching all of her older brothers attend college, Stone decided that she wanted to attend as well, in spite of her parents' wishes. In 1839, Stone attended Mount Holyoke Seminary for one term, then enrolled in Oberlin College in Ohio four years later. Oberlin was considered a progressive institution at the time; however, they did not give Stone the opportunity to pursue public speaking because of her sex. Stone graduated with honors in 1847, becoming the first woman to earn a bachelor's degree in Massachusetts.

Through her connection with William Lloyd Garrison, whom she had met at Oberlin, Stone began to work with the American Anti-Slavery Society. This launched her career as a public speaker. She faced much backlash for her work as an abolitionist and women's rights activist, even being excommunicated by the Congregational Church.

In 1850, Stone held the first national Women's Rights Convention in Worcester, Massachusetts. Her speech at the convention was recorded in newspapers all over the country. For the next few years, Stone traveled through North America, lecturing on women's rights, and she continued to hold the Convention every year.

In 1855, Stone married Henry Blackwell, a fellow abolitionist and activist who had been asking to marry her for two years. She took her husband's name at first but decided to go back. She stated, "A wife should no more take her husband's name than he should take hers. My name is my identity and must not be lost." At their wedding, she and Blackwell both protested the idea of signing a document stating that a man has legal control over his wife. The couple eventually moved to Orange, New Jersey and gave birth to a daughter, Alice Stone Blackwell.

Stone cofounded and became president of the New Jersey Woman Suffrage Association in 1868, then launched a New England chapter of the Association and helped found the American Equal Rights Association.

"I think, with never-ending gratitude, that the young women of today do not and can never know at what price their right to free speech and to speak at all in public has been earned." — Lucy Stone

After the Civil War, Stone found herself at odds with her former allies, Elizabeth Cady Stanton and Susan B. Anthony. They opposed the fifteenth amendment, which only allowed black men the right to vote and not women, while Stone supported it, her reasoning being that it would eventually lead to the women's vote as well. Stanton and Anthony felt that Stone was betraying the women's movement, and the movement was divided into factions. In 1880, the movement was reunified, thanks largely to Stone's daughter, Alice, and Stanton's daughter, Harriet Stanton Blanch. This is when the National American Woman Suffrage Association was born.

Lucy Stone was able to see the end of slavery, but died on October 18, 1893 in Dorchester, Massachusetts, thirty years before women were finally given the right to vote. Her ashes are held at a columbarium in Forest Hill Cemetery in Boston.

Jane Addams

J ane Addams (born Laura Jane Addams) was born in Cedarville, Illinois on September 6, 1860. She was the eighth of nine children born to John H. and Sarah Addams. Her father was a businessman and state senator and the family lived a life of privilege. Her father was friends with many powerful people, including Abraham Lincoln.

Addams graduated from the Rockford Female Seminary in Illinois in 1881, then briefly attended medical school. At the age of twenty-seven, while traveling with her friend Ellen Gates Starr, she visited Tonybee Hall in London, an institution established to help the poor. The two friends were so impressed that they decided to open a similar establishment in Chicago. In 1889, they opened Hull House, named after the building's first owner. There they provided help for the poor population of the Chicago area. The organization grew over the years, and eventually included more than ten buildings, and it had educational services, child care, an art gallery, a kitchen, and other social programs.

In 1905, Addams began serving on the Chicago Board of Education. Five years later she became the first female president of the National Conference of Charities and Corrections, which was later renamed the National Conference of Social Work. The following year, she established the National Federation of Settlements, and she headed it for the following two decades.

Addams was a committed pacifist and peace activist and a frequent lecturer on the subject. In 1907, she published her speeches on ending war in *Newer Ideals of Peace*. During World War I she became chair of the Women's Peace Party. She attended the International Congress of Women in the Netherlands in 1915, along with Emily Greene Balch and Alice Hamilton. The three women worked together to write *Women at The Hague: The International Congress of Women and Its Results*, and it was published that same year.

"Nothing could be worse than the fear that one had given up too soon and left one unexpected effort that might have saved the world." — Jane Addams

From 1919 to 1929, Addams served as president of the Women's International League for Peace and Freedom. In 1931 she shared the Nobel Peace Prize with Nicholas Murray Butler, presidential advisor and educator.

Addams's health had always been delicate, but it began to seriously decline after she had a heart attack in 1926. She died on May 21, 1935, at the age of seventy-four, in Chicago.

Concepcion Arenal

Concepcion Arenal was born January 31, 1820 in Gallicia, Spain. Her father was a military officer named Angel del Arenal, who was often imprisoned for his liberal political ideologies and opposition to the regime of Ferdinand VII. He became ill in prison and died in 1829, when Concepcion was eight. She moved to Armano with her mother, and then to Madrid in 1834, where she attended the school of the Count of Tepa. In 1841, she entered the Faculty of Law of the Central University (now the Complutense University of Madrid). She was the first woman to attend University in Spain. She graduated in 1848 and married Fernando Garcia Carrasco, a writer and lawyer. They had three children together, a daughter who died shortly after birth, and two sons, Fernando and Ramon.

Arenal and her husband collaborated on and published the newspaper *Iberia* until Fernando died in 1859. She was forced to sell everything she owned and moved into the home of violinist and composer Jesus de Monasterio in Potes, Cantabria. The same year she founded a feminist group, Conference of Saint Vincent de Paul, to help the poor. Two years later she was awarded La beneficencia, la filantropia y la caridad (Beneficence, philanthropy and charity) prize from the Academy of Moral Sciences. She was the first woman to ever receive it.

Arenal wrote several books of poetry and essays over the years, such as *Letters to Delinquents, Ode Against Slavery*, and *Execution of the Death Sentence*. She supported prison reform and better conditions for prisoners, and in 1868 was named Inspector of Women's Correctional Houses. In 1869, she wrote *The Woman of the Future*, a book that critiqued the belief that women were biologically inferior to men. In 1872, she founded the Construction Beneficiary, an organization devoted to providing cheap housing for laborers. She worked for the Red Cross, becoming the Secretary General in 1871-72.

Arenel argued for women's right to any level of education, but she didn't believe that women should be in positions of power or authority, or involvement in politics, because she believed that it could lead to women neglecting their families. She was still the leading voice of the feminist movement at the time, when gender roles were very traditional in Spain. Her work was focused on the most marginalized people of society, and she wrote extensively about the state of women and men's prisons and women's place in society. Her work *Domestic Service* is what made her known as the founder of the feminist movement in Spain.

" . . . a serious mistake, and one of the most harmful, to impress upon women that her sole mission is to be wife and mother; it amounts to tell her that she can be nothing by herself and to annihilate her moral and intellectual self." — Concepcion Arenel

Arenel died February 4, 1893 in Vigo. A statue of her has been erected in Madrid.

Elizabeth Garrett Anderson

Elizabeth Garrett was born June 9, 1836 in east London, one of the twelve children of Newson and Louisa Garret. Her father was a pawnbroker, and he became a successful businessman and was able to send all of his children to good schools. When she was done with school, Garrett was expected to get married, have children, and live the life of a lady, but meeting with feminist Emily Davies and Elizabeth Blackwell, the first female doctor in the United States, led to her decision to become a doctor.

When she was denied access to several different medical schools, she enrolled as a nursing student at Middlesex Hospital. There she attended classes for male doctors but was banned when other students complained. The Society of Apothecaries rules did not specifically state that women could not take the exams, and in 1865 she passed her exams, earning a certificate that allowed her to be a doctor. Unfortunately, the Society of Apothecaries changed the rules so that other women could not earn their certificate the same way.

In 1866, with her father's help, she established a dispensary for women in London and in 1870 was made a visiting physician at the East London Hospital. Here she met James Anderson, a successful businessman, who she married in 1871. The couple had three children.

Anderson still had not been able to earn her medical degree and was determined to do so, so she taught herself French and attended the University of Paris, where she finally earned her degree, which the British Medical Register refused to recognize.

Anderson founded the New Hospital for Women in London in 1872 (Later it was renamed after its founder.). The hospital was staffed entirely by women. Anderson appointed Elizabeth Blackwell as the professor of gynecology there.

Anderson paved the way for other women to study medicine. In 1876 an act was passed that permitted women to enter medical professions. In 1883, Anderson was appointed dean of the London School of Medicine for women, which she helped to found in 1874.

In 1902, Anderson retired to Aldeburgh, a town on the Suffolk coast. In 1908, she became mayor of the town and was the first female mayor in England. Both Anderson and her daughter Louisa were prominent in the Suffrage movement. She died on December 17, 1917.

Princess Louise Duchess of Argyll

P rincess Louisa (mostly known as Louise) was born March 18, 1848 in Buckingham Palace, London. She was the sixth child and fourth daughter of Queen Victoria and Prince Albert. Victoria's labor with Louise was the first to be assisted by the use of chloroform. She spent her childhood in various royal residences with her family. She and her siblings were strictly educated, and were also taught practical skills such as cooking, farming, and carpentry. Of her daughter, Queen Victoria said, "She was born in the most eventful of times and ought to be something peculiar in consequence." This statement probably had to do with Louise's determined and somewhat rebellious temperament. Louise was a sculptor and artist, and some of her sculptures remain today. Because she was royalty, a career in the arts was out of the question, but her mother did allow her to be tutored by sculptor Mary Thornycroft, and in 1863 allowed her to attend The National Art Training School. She was possibly the most intelligent of her siblings, making her a favorite of her father's.

After her father died on December 14, 1861, Louisa worked as an unofficial secretary to her mother, and the court went into a prolonged state of mourning. Louisa quickly became frustrated and bored with the lack of entertainment, and her mother considered her to be difficult. Louisa then fell in love with her brother's tutor, Robinson Duckworth between 1866 and 1870, and the queen reacted by dismissing Duckworth.

In the late 1860s her marriage began to be discussed. (The press accused her of multiple affairs, and her support of the feminist movement was also noted.) She was acquainted with women such as Josephine Butler and Elizabeth Garrett. She had royal suitors from Denmark and Prussia, but none of them suited her, and none suited the queen. Louise didn't want to marry any prince and announced that she was in love with John Campbell, Marquess of Lorne, heir to the Duke of Argyll. Although many in the royal family opposed the match, Victoria eventually gave the couple her blessing, saying that bringing "new blood" into the royal family would strengthen them. They were married on March 21, 1871.

In 1878, Lorne was chosen to be the Governor General of Canada, and Louise became his Viceregal Consort. She used her new position to support the arts and higher education and also the feminist cause. Louise and Lorne founded the Royal Canadian Academy of the Arts and Louise served as patroness of the Ladies' Educational Association, the Women's Protective Immigration Society, and the Society of Decorative Arts. In 1905 Alberta was named after Princess Louisa Caroline Alberta, as well as Lake Louise and Mount Alberta.

The couple returned to England in 1883. Louise and Lorne's relationship was strained, and they often were not under the same roof. Rumors began to spread that Lorne was a homosexual. More rumors surfaced about Louise, saying that she had an affair with Arthur Bigge, then later Lord Stamfordham. Louise denied the rumors, saying they were started by her sisters, with whom her relationship was strained at best. She was later romantically linked by the press with several other men.

While Queen Victoria was against women entering professions, Louise continued to support the suffrage movement. She was always liberal minded, along with her eldest sister, Victoria. Louise was also known for her generosity and charity to servants.

Queen Victoria died on January 22, 1901, leaving Kent House to Louise. Louise's brother, Edward VII, became king.

On May 2, 1914, Lorne died of pneumonia. Louise suffered a nervous breakdown and was intensely lonely without the duke. Her last public appearance was in 1937 at the Home Arts and Industries Exhibition. She died at Kensington Palace, December 3, 1939.

Helen Keller

Helen Keller was the firstborn daughter of Arthur H. Keller and Katherine Adams Keller. She had another sister as well as two stepbrothers. Their father served in the Confederacy during the Civil War. The family owned a cotton plantation but were not considered wealthy. Later on, Arthur became the publisher of the local newspaper the *North Alabamian*.

In 1882, Helen developed an illness, called a "brain fever" by the family doctor, although experts today speculate that it could have been scarlet fever or meningitis. A few days after the fever broke, Katherine realized that Helen wasn't responding to the dinner bell or notice when a hand was waved in front of her face. At nineteen months old, the child had lost both her sight and her hearing.

As a child, Helen created a type of sign language to communicate with her companion, Martha Washington, who was the daughter of the family's cook. They had more than sixty signs that they used to communicate with each other. Despite this, Helen had grown quite wild; she would fly into rages, kicking and screaming when she was angry or upset and giggling uncontrollably when she was happy. Some family members began suggesting that she should be institutionalized.

In 1886, Keller's mother came across a work by Charles Dickens, *American Notes,* in which she read about the education of another deaf and blind child named Laura Bridgman. She sent Keller and her father to Baltimore to see a specialist named Dr. J. Julian Chisolm. Chisolm examined Keller and recommended that she see the inventor of the telephone, Alexander Graham Bell, who had been working with deaf children. After meeting with the family, Bell suggested that they travel to Massachusetts in order to visit the Perkins Institute for the Blind in Boston. The family then met with the school's director, Michael Anaganos, who suggested that Keller work with one of the institutes recent graduates, Anne Sullivan. Thus began a forty-nine year relationship between Keller and Sullivan.

"Science may have found a cure for most evils; but it has found no remedy for the worst of them all—the apathy of human beings." — Helen Keller

Sullivan went to the Kellers' home on March 3, 1887. She began work right away, gifting Helen a doll and then teaching her the finger spelling for the word doll. Keller was defiant and difficult to work with. Even when she did cooperate, Sullivan could see that she wasn't making the connection between the finger spelling and the words and objects they were supposed to represent. Keller became more and more frustrated and would continuously fly into rages. Sullivan eventually demanded that she and Keller isolate themselves from the rest of the family for a while. They moved to a nearby cottage on the plantation.

One day Sullivan was trying to teach Keller the word for water. She put one of Keller's hands under the pump and moved the lever to create a flow of water, and spelled out the word into her other hand. Keller finally made the connection and spelled w-a-t-e-r into Sullivan's hand. She touched the ground, wanting to know its name.

Sullivan taught her the word. By the end of the day, Helen had learned thirty words.

Helen began taking speech classes at the Horace Mann School for the Deaf in Boston in 1890. For twenty-five years she worked to learn to speak so that people could understand her. Then she attended the Wright-Humason School for the Deaf in New York City. She worked on improving her communication skills as well as study academic subjects. In 1869, Keller began studying at the Cambridge School for Young Ladies. Her story began to be known throughout the country, and she met many famous people, including author Mark Twain. The two became friends, and he introduced her to Henry H. Rogers, a Standard Oil Executive. Rogers was so impressed by her that he decided to pay for her to attend Radcliffe College. Sullivan accompanied her there in order to interpret lectures and reading. Keller wrote her first book, *The Story of My Life*, with the help of Sullivan and her future husband, John Macy. Keller, had by this time mastered Braille, finger spelling, typing, and touch lip reading. Keller graduated, cum laude, from Radcliffe at the age of twenty-four in 1904.

A year later, Sullivan married John Macy, a Harvard professor and prominent socialist. Keller went on to live with the couple, but their marriage began to fail, possibly because of Anne's devotion and attention to Helen, and the couple separated after several years, though they never divorced.

Keller soon became a celebrity and gave lectures on her experiences. She worked on behalf of others with disabilities and also became an advocate of women's suffrage and birth control. She co-founded Helen Keller International along with city planner George Kessler in 1915, to combat issues like blindness and malnutrition. In 1920 she helped found the American Civil Liberties Union.

Keller was a member of the Socialist Party and supported socialist presidential candidate Eugene Debs. She wrote several articles about socialism and published her essays, titled *Out of the Dark*. Up until this point, she had been portrayed positively in the press, but now that she was speaking out on her socialist views she received some backlash, some even calling attention to her disabilities.

In 1932, Anne Sullivan became completely blind. She had been experiencing health problems and died in 1936. Sullivan and Keller's secretary, Polly Thomson, now became Keller's companion.

Keller traveled to thirty-five countries between 1946 and 1957. At the age of seventy-five, in 1955, Keller went on a forty-thousand-mile, five-month trip through Asia. She reached and inspired millions of people through her speeches and lectures.

Keller died on June 1, 1968, a few weeks shy of her eightieth-eight birthday.

Emily Davies

Emily Davies was born in Gateshead in 1830, one of four children of Reverend John Davies and Mary Hopkinson. She had three brothers, who were all sent to boarding school while she was educated at home. She was close with her oldest brother, John Llewelyn, who was educated at Cambridge. Emily was very aware that she had been denied an equal education with that of her brothers.

Davies was involved with several other feminists of the time, meeting Elizabeth Garrett in 1854 at the home of her friends Jane and Emily Crow. Elizabeth went on to introduce Emily to Barbara Leigh Smith and Bessie Parkes. Possibly inspired by Garrett, Emily toyed with the idea of studying medicine, but didn't think that her early education was sufficient enough to make this possible. Instead she decided to devote her life to higher education for women, helping to give them the opportunities that she had been denied as a young woman. She campaigned to have women allowed into Cambridge, Oxford, and London University. The Schools Enquiry Association agreed to look into gender inequalities in education in 1864. Davies went on to write her book, *The Higher Education of Women*.

In 1865, Davies joined with Elizabeth Garret Anderson, Barbara Bodichon, Dorothea Beale, and Francis Mary Buss to form the Kensington Society, a women's discussion group. A year later the group formed the London Suffrage Committee and began to petition Parliament to grant women the right to vote. However, Davies soon disagreed with most of the members of this group, who wanted to grant women the vote on the same terms as men, while Davies thought they would have more chance of success if they only asked for unmarried women to be able to vote. After this rift, Davies did not play a significant role in the suffrage movement for the next twenty years. She focused instead on creating a women's college, with the help of Barbara Bodichon and other feminists. Davies raised enough money to purchase a house two miles outside of Cambridge called Benslow. In 1873 the house was opened as Girton College. The students there would not be admitted full membership to the University of Cambridge until 1948.

"If neither mother nor governess knows, how can they teach? So long as education is not provided for them, how can it be provided by them?" — Sarah Emily Davies

Davies's ideas on education were more conservative than the liberal Barbara Bodichon. Davies believed that students should focus on classical subjects, while Bodichon was more radical leaning. They also clashed when it came to disciplining students, Davies being the stricter of the two. Davies also insisted that the college be affiliated with the Church of England.

In 1889, Davies joined the London National Society for Women's Suffrage and also the National Union of Suffrage Societies, but got into disagreements here, too. She didn't agree with the suffragettes' militant tactics, and she didn't believe that all adults should have the right to vote. In 1912 she resigned when the NUSS decided to fully support the Labour Party. She then joined the Conservative and Unionists Women's Franchise Society.

By 1919, Davies was one of the only early members of the Women's Suffrage Society alive to vote in the Parliamentary election. She died in 1921.

Barbara Bodichon

Barbara Bodichon was born in Sussex in 1827 to parents Benjamin Leigh Smith and Anne Longden. Her father came from a radical unitarian family. Her grandfather worked in Parliament with William Wilberforce in his campaign against the slave trade and was a supporter of the French Revolution, and her great-grandfather had sided with the American colonists over the British government. The family was also related to Fanny Smith, mother of Florence Nightingale.

At the time of Barbara's birth, her father was a member of the House of Commons and her mother was a seventeeen-year-old milliner. The birth created a scandal because the couple never married, Anne remaining his common-law wife until her death of tuberculosis when Barbara was seven. Some members of Benjamin's family urged him to have his children brought up abroad after Anne's death, but their father brought them up himself, first in Hastings and then at his home in London.

Benjamin Leigh Smith's home was a meeting place for radicals and political refugees. This exposed Barbara to a wide range of people involved in politics from a young age. Barbara's father was an advocate for women's rights and brought her and her sisters up in the same way as he did her brothers. Barbara and her four siblings attended a local school where they were educated among working class children.

Benjamin Leigh Smith gave each of his children three hundred pounds a year when they turned twenty-one. It was unusual for fathers to treat their daughters this way, and it gave Barbara a chance at independence. She used some of the money to establish her own school in London. She selected Elizabeth Whitehead to be the headteacher of the school, which later became known as the Portman Hall School. The idea was to create a school that was undenominational, co-educational, and for children of all different backgrounds.

"I hope there are some who will brave ridicule for the sake of common justice to half the people of the world." — Barbara Bodichon

In the 1850s, Barbara gave evidence to a House of Commons committee that was looking into the legal position of married women. This led to the creation of the Matrimonial Causes Act, which allowed divorce through court of law rather than the slow and expensive process through a Private Act of Parliament. This act also protected the property rights of divorced women.

Barbara was critical of the legal system at the time, which specifically failed to protect the property and earnings of married women. She wrote *Women and Work* in 1857, arguing that a woman's dependence on her husband was degrading. As a young woman, Barbara had fallen in love with John Chapmen, editor of the *Westminster Review,* but wouldn't marry him because of the legal position of married women. After meeting Eugene Bodichon, she compromised her principles by marrying him. Bodichon also held radical views and supported Barbara while she campaigned for women's rights.

In 1858, Barbara and her friend Bessie Rayner Parkes founded *The Englishwoman's Review.* The journal campaigned for female doctors and higher education for women. In 1866, she formed the first Women's Suffrage Committee. The Committee organized the women's suffrage petition, which was presented to the House of Commons by John Stuart Mill on their behalf. Bodichon traveled the country holding meetings for women's suffrage, and her speeches converted many women to the cause, including Lydia Becker, a future leader of the movement. She also continued to work on improving women's education, joining Emily Davies to raise funds for the first women's college in Cambridge.

In 1877 Bodichon became seriously ill and was left paralyzed. After this, she was no longer able to take an active role in the women's rights movement. She died June 11, 1891, leaving a large sum of money to Girton College.

Dorothea Beale

D orothea Beale was born March 21, 1831 to parents Miles Beale and Dorothea Complin. Her father was a surgeon and employed a governess for his eleven children. Dorothea went to school in Paris for a year when she was sixteen. She became a student at Queen's College for Women in 1848 when it first opened. When she finished her studies, she was appointed the first female mathematics tutor. She later became dissatisfied with the school and became head teacher at Casterton School, however she left a year later after a failed attempt to change the way the school was organized.

After leaving Casterton School she focused on writing a *Textbook of General History*, which became popular with teachers. She was then appointed head teacher of Cheltenham Ladies College. Under her leadership it became one of the most highly regarded schools in the country. Rather than focusing on music and drawing, like most schools for women at the time, Dorothea focused on a broader range of academic subjects. She was involved in trying to improve the national standard of education and was a part of the Head Mistresses' Guild and the Teachers' Guild.

"I would earnestly press on all my readers, that their own education must never be regarded as finished; if we cease to learn, we lose the power of sympathy with our pupils, and a teacher without intellectual and moral sympathy has no dynamic, no inspiring force." — Dorothea Beale

In 1865, Dorothea joined with Elizabeth Garrett, Emily Davies and eight other women to form the Kensington Society, a discussion group for women. The group drafted a petition to Parliament asking to grant women the right to vote. John Stuart Mill added an amendment to the 1867 Reform Act that would have given women the same rights as men, but the amendment lost the vote. After this the Kensington Society decided to form the London Society for Women's Suffrage. Dorothea later became vice president of the Central Society for Women's Suffrage.

In 1892, Beale purchased Cowley House in Oxford, opening it as St. Hilda's College a year later. She wrote several books about educating women, including *Work and Play in Girls' Schools* in 1898. She continued working as the principal at Cheltenham Ladies College until her death on November 9, 1906.

Frances Buss

Frances Buss was born August 16, 1827, daughter of Robert Buss and Frances Fleetwood. Frances was the eldest of ten children, only five of which survived into adulthood. Her father was an engraver, but was unsuccessful and the family was extremely poor.

Frances attended a local public school. She did very well there, and when she was fourteen she was asked to help the teacher with the other children. Mrs. Buss was inspired by her daughter to open her own school, and gave Frances the job of teaching the older children. Frances wanted to improve her teaching methods and became a night student at the recently opened Queen's College in 1849. By 1850, Frances had opened her own school, the North London Collegiate School for Girls, only employing qualified teachers. The school soon developed an excellent reputation. Frances had lecturers visit from Queen's College, as well as other women who were trying to improve education for women. This included Emily Davies, and the two women became close friends and both became involved in the campaign to allow women at Oxford and Cambridge. In 1864, the Schools Enquiry Commission agreed to look into gender

inequalities in education, and in 1865, Frances gave evidence to the Commission. The same year, she joined the Kensington Society, a discussion group for women. The following year the group formed the London Suffrage Committee. Frances remained a supporter of universal suffrage throughout her life, as well as working with Josephine Butler in her campaigns against the white slave trade and the Contagious Diseases Act.

In 1871, Buss took the step of changing the North London Collegiate School from a private school to an endowed grammar school. This resulted in a loss of income, but Buss wanted to be able to offer a good education to girls whose families could not afford private school.

In 1880, Frances began to suffer from kidney disease. She continued to run the North London Collegiate School until her death on December 24, 1894.

Harriet Taylor

Harriet Taylor was born October 8, 1807 in Walworth. She was the daughter of Thomas Hardy, a London surgeon, and his wife Harriet Hurst. She married John Taylor, a wealthy businessman from Islington, at the age of eighteen. Over the next few years she had two sons and a daughter, Helen Taylor.

John and Harriet Taylor both became involved in the Unitarian Church and developed radical politics. They were friends with William Johnson Fox, a Unitarian minister and supporter of women's rights.

In 1830, Harriet met the philosopher John Stuart Mill. He was the first man who had ever treated Harriet as an intellectual equal. She was attracted to him, and he was so impressed with her that he asked her to read and comment on his latest book. The two went on to exchange essays on issues like marriage and women's rights. Harriet seems to have held more radical views that Mill on these subjects. She was drawn to socialism, and read books by Robert Owen such as *The Formation of Character* and *A New View of Society*, and she was especially critical of women's economic dependence on men. She believed it was degrading and argued for a total reform of all marriage laws.

In 1833, Harriet separated from her husband, then spent six weeks with John Stuart Mill in Paris. She then moved to a house at Walton-on-Thames where Mill visited her on the weekends. They maintained that they were not having an affair, but their friends were all scandalized, and the couple became socially isolated. John Roebuck is later quoted saying, "My affection for Mill was so warm and so sincere that I was hurt by anything which brought ridicule upon him. I saw, or thought I saw, how mischievous might be this affair, and as we had become in all things like brothers, I determined, most unwisely, to speak to him on the subject. With this resolution I went to the India House next day, and then frankly told him what I thought might result from his connection with Mrs. Taylor. He received my warnings coldly, and after some time I took my leave, little thinking what effect my remonstrances had produced. The next day I again called at the India House. The moment I entered the room I saw that, as far he was concerned, our friendship was at an end. His manner was not merely cold, but repulsive; and I, seeing how matters were, left him. His part of our friendship was rooted out, nay, destroyed, but mine was untouched."

> "Public offices being open to them alike, all occupations would be divided between the sexes in their natural arrangements. Fathers would provide for their daughters in the same manner as their sons." — Harriet Taylor

Harriet published very little of her own writing during her lifetime, except for a few articles in *Monthly Repository*, a Unitarian journal. However, Mill stated in his autobiography that Harriet was coauthor of most of the books and articles that he had published under his own name, adding "when two persons have their thoughts and speculations completely in common it is of little consequence in respect of the question of originality, which of them holds the pen."

John Taylor died of cancer on May 3, 1849, but Harriet was still so concerned with creating a scandal that she insisted that she and Mill wait two years before getting married.

Harriet and Mill both suffered from tuberculosis. In November of 1858, Harriet died while seeking treatment for her condition. At the time of her death, she and Mill had been working on a book called *The Subjugation of Women*, and Harriet's daughter Helen now helped Mill finish the book. The two worked together for the next fifteen years.

Bessie Rayner Parkes

Bessie Rayner Belloc was born June 16, 1829. She was the daughter of solicitor Joseph Parkes, and granddaughter of Joseph Priestly, a scientist and political reformer who was forced to leave the country in 1774. Bessie's father was a Unitarian and was close friends with John Stuart Mill and Henry Brougham.

In 1846, Bessie met Barbara Bodichon, who was running a progressive school in London. The two women became close friends, and they published several pamphlets on women's rights over the next few years, including *Remarks on the Education of Girls* in 1856. In 1858, they started *The Englishwoman's Review*, a journal for educated women. Bessie became the editor and made the journal available to writers campaigning for equal opportunities for women. In 1866, Parkes and Bodichon formed the first Women's Suffrage Committee.

While visiting France in 1867, Bessie met Louis Belloc. The couple soon fell in love and decided to get married, however both families objected to the marriage. Belloc was younger than Bessie, and she had been an invalid for thirteen years. Even Bodichon advised against it, but the marriage went ahead anyway. The couple had two children.

Louis Belloc died of sunstroke in 1872, and Bessie retuned to London with her children. She was no longer a part of the Unitarian Church, having abandoned it for the Roman Catholic Church. She was also no longer involved in women's rights. Her daughter, Marie Belloc-Lowndes, was a successful writer, but showed no interest in the women's rights movement, and her son was actually an anti-feminist, opposed to women having the vote and getting a higher education. Parkes died March 23, 1925.

"What do the scales of Justice hold,
Poised even in that steady hand?—
What is that measure closely scanned?"
—Bessie Rayner Parkes

Josephine Butler

J osephine Butler was born April 13, 1828, daughter of John Grey and Hannah Annett. Her father, a wealthy landowner, was a supporter of social reform and campaigned for the 1832 Reform Act. Josephine learned to dislike inequality and injustice.

Prince Leopold was quoted saying that Josephine was "considered by many people to be the most beautiful woman in the world." In 1852, she married George Butler, an examiner of schools in Oxford. Over the next five years, Josephine had five children. In 1867, the family moved when George became vice-principal of Cheltenham College. The couple experiences a great deal of hostility at Cheltenham when they made their support for the anti-slavery movement known.

In 1836, Josephine's only daughter, Eva, fell to her death. Josephine was devastated and never fully recovered. After this, Josephine became involved in charity work, visiting the local workhouse and helping prostitutes get off the streets. She also began to take an interest in women's education. She joined with Anne Jemima Clough in 1867, establishing advanced study courses for women. That same year, Josephine was appointed president of the North of England Council for Higher Education of Women. In 1868, she became involved in a campaign to persuade Cambridge University to provide more opportunities for female students. This led to the establishment of Newnham College.

The same year, Josephine published her book, *The Education and Employment of Women*, in which she argued for improved education and equal opportunities for women. In 1869, she published *Women's Work and Women's Culture*, in which she said that women should not "try to rival men since they had a different part to play in society." This was upsetting to some other feminists. Butler believed that women were different from men and that their purpose was to care for the weak, and that women's suffrage was important to the welfare of the nation.

In 1869, Josephine began campaigning against the Contagious Diseases Act, which had been introduced in the 1860s as a way to reduce venereal disease in the armed forces. Josephine objected to the laws that only applied to women because under these laws, police could arrest any women they believed to be prostitutes and then force them to get medically examined. Josephine toured the country making speeches criticizing the CDA. She was a skilled orator and attracted huge audiences, but many people were shocked to hear a woman speak publicly about sexual matters. Her husband was criticized for allowing his wife to become so involved in the campaign, but he continued to support her efforts.

"It is a fact, that numbers even of moral and religious people have permitted themselves to accept and condone in man what is fiercely condemned in woman." — Josephine Butler

Butler was very sympathetic to the plight of prostitutes, and she became involved in a campaign against child prostitution. In 1885 Butler joined with Florence Booth of the Salvation Army and W.T. Stead, editor of the *Pall Mall Gazette*, to expose what was known as the white slave trade. The group used the example of Eliza Armstrong, a girl who at the age of thirteen had been bought for five pounds by a woman working for a London brothel. The case gained so much publicity that Parliament passed the Criminal Law Amendment Act, which raised the age of consent from thirteen to sixteen.

The CDA was repealed in 1886, after which Josephine spent her time caring for her sick husband. He died in 1890, and Josephine wrote *Recollections of George Butler* in 1892 and *Personal Reminiscences of a Great Crusade* in 1896. In the last few years of her life, she supported the National Union of Suffrage Societies. Josephine Butler died on December 30, 1906.

Anne Clough

Anne Clough was born January 20, 1820, the third child of James Clough and Anne Perfect. She was born in Liverpool, but the family moved to Charleston, South Carolina for a few years after she was born. When the family returned to Liverpool in 1836, James Clough became a cotton merchant.

After her father's business failed in 1841, Anne opened a small school in Liverpool to help her family out of debt. The school opened in 1842, but attracted few children. In 1852, Anne moved to the village of Ambleside and opened a local school for the children of farmers and tradespeople. The school was popular and Anne soon had to employ two more teachers. She gave up the school when her brother, Arthur Hough Clough died. Anne's achievements, however, were well known, and in 1864 Emily Davies, who was involved in improving women's education, contacted her. Clough was encouraged by Davies and wrote the article "Hints on the Organization of Girls' Schools" for *Macmillan's Magazine*. In 1865, Anne joined the Kensington Society, a discussion group for women.

Anne was inspired by the successes of the North London Collegiate School and Cheltenham Ladies College and decided to form the North of England Council for Promoting the Higher Education of Women. Some members included Josephine Butler, George Butler, and Elizabeth Wolstenholme, and the first meeting was held in Leeds in 1867.

After it was established in 1871, Anne was invited to take charge Newnham, a residence for women who were attending lectures at Cambridge University. As well as being principal there, Anne helped to establish the University Association of Assistant Mistresses, the Cambridge Training College for Women, and the Women's University Settlement in Southwark. Anne Clough died February 27, 1892.

Elizabeth Wolstenholme-Elmy

E lizabeth Wolstenholme was born December 15, 1833, daughter of a Methodist minister, Joseph Wolstenholme, and his wife, Elizabeth Clarke. Elizabeth's brother Joseph received an expensive formal education and eventually became professor of mathematics at Cambridge University, but their father had a traditional view of education for women, and Elizabeth only received two years of formal education.

After the death of both of her parents, her new guardians refused to permit her to attend the newly opened Bedford College for Women. Elizabeth continued to educate herself at home until she received her inheritance at nineteen. In 1853, she purchased her own girls' boarding school in Worsley, Lancashire. In 1865, Elizabeth joined with other female schoolteachers in the area to form the Manchester Schoolmistresses' Association. Two years later, Elizabeth joined with Josephine Butler to establish the North of England Council for the Higher Education of Women, which provided lectures and examinations for women who wanted to become teachers. In 1869, Butler asked Elizabeth to contribute an article for her book *Women's Work and Women's Culture*. In the article, she criticized parents' lack of interest in their daughters' education.

After the Contagious Diseases Act was passed in 1864, Butler and Elizabeth formed the Ladies National Association for the Repeal of the Contagious Diseases Acts. They believed that it would be impossible to have sexist laws like this repealed unless women were allowed to vote.

In 1868, Elizabeth became secretary of the Married Women's Property Committee. Their goal was to change the common law doctrine to include the wife's right to buy, sell, and own her separate property. Elizabeth worked with Josephine Butler and Richard Pankhurst on the executive committee of the organization.

In the early 1870s, Elizabeth met and became friends with Benjamin Elmy, a poet for Congleton. Elizabeth became pregnant with his child in 1874. Some members of the Married Women's Property Committee wanted Elizabeth to resign because of the scandal she had caused, saying that it could harm the women's movement. Josephine Butler defended the couple, saying, "They have sinned against no law of Purity. They went through a most solemn ceremony and vow before witnesses. I knew of this true marriage before God—early in 1874. It would have been a legal marriage in Scotland. They blundered; but their whole action was grave and pure. The English marriage laws are impure. English law . . . sins against the law of purity. It is a species of legal prostitution, the woman being the man's property." Another member of the committee, Lydia Becker, resigned.

Elizabeth married Elmy while pregnant at the Kensington Register Office in October of 1874. Elizabeth stayed true to her principles, however, refusing to promise obedience to her husband, wear a wedding ring, or change her surname. A few months later she gave birth to a son.

In 1889, Elizabeth, along with Richard Pankhurst, Emmeline Pankhurst, and Ursula Bright, formed the Women's Franchise League. Elizabeth and the Pankhursts were members of the Independent Labor Party, but Bright was a member of the Liberal Party and Elizabeth found herself constantly at odds with her. Eventually she resigned the Franchise League after another argument with Bright, stating she did "not intend ever again to take any part whatever in political action on behalf of women." However, within the year she established another suffrage group, the Women's Emancipation Union.

In the early 1900s Elizabeth was one of the first people to join the Women's Social and Political Union, after becoming critical of the National Union of Women's Suffrage Societies. She was by this time in her seventies and was not able to take direct action that could have landed her in prison. She wrote, "I am old and hope many mornings that the end may be soon and sudden—and indeed I am so tired in the brain, head and body, that I long for rest." In March of 1906, Elizabeth's husband died.

Elizabeth was concerned about the WSPU's increasing use of violence, but unlike many other members, she refused to resign. She died at the age of eighty-four on March 12, 1918 in a Manchester nursing home.

Louisa Martindale

Louisa Martindale was born in 1839. She was the eldest daughter of James Spicer and Louisa Edwards. Her father owned a wholesale paper business, and Louisa was raised as a Congregationalist, along with her nine siblings.

After finishing school, Louisa became involved in charity work, helping to form a Mutual Improvement Society and a Congregationalist Sunday School. She also became interested in the women's movement around this time.

In 1871, Louisa married William Martindale, a widower with four children of his own. Over the next four years, Louisa had two daughters, Louisa (1873) and Hilda (1875). After the death of her husband, the family moved to Lewes in Sussex.

Louisa is known to have read the book *A Vindication of the Rights of Women* by Mary Wollstonecraft. She agreed with Wollstonecraft that girls should have the same academic opportunities as boys. However, at the time there were very few schools for girls. Louisa tried to start her own school in Lewes, but received so much backlash that she decided to give up the project entirely. She moved to Brighton in 1885 so that her daughters could attend the Brighton High School for Girls.

After settling in Brighton, Louisa became active in politics. She was a member of Brighton's Women's Co-operative Guild and wrote several pamphlets on the women's movement. Louisa also helped start a Brighton branch of the Suffrage Society and another suffrage group within the Liberal Federation.

Louisa set up a women's dispensary in Brighton with the help of her daughters and other feminists in the area. She raised enough money to build the New Sussex Hospital for Women. Louisa Martindale died in 1914.

Margaret Bondfield

Margaret Bondfield, daughter of William Bondfield and Anne Taylor, was born March 17, 1873. Margaret was Anne's eleventh child. Her father had worked in the textile industry since he was a boy, and he was well known for his radical political beliefs. From a young age, Margaret had read widely about social issues.

At the age of fourteen, Margaret left her home in Chard, Somerset to apprentice in a draper's shop in Hove. She later said, "When I first went to Brighton for a holiday in 1887 I had the chance of a job as an apprentice to Mrs. White of Church Road, Hove, a friend of my sister Anne. I eagerly grasped this opportunity of earning my living. I did not see my home again for five years. Mrs. White successfully ran one of those old-fashioned businesses where the relations between the customer and assistant were of the most courteous and friendly, and the assistants, of whom I was the youngest, were treated like members of the family." It was here that Margaret became friends with a customer, Louisa Martindale, a women's rights advocate. She was a frequent visitor at Louisa's house and borrowed books from her.

Margaret went to live with her brother Frank in London in 1894. She quickly found work in a shop and was soon elected to the Shop Assistants Union District Council. In 1896, Clementina Black of the Women's Industrial Council asked Margaret to investigate the pay and working conditions of shop workers. The report was published in 1898, and that same year she was appointed assistant secretary of the Shop Assistants' Union.

Margaret wrote in her autobiography, "I concentrated on my job. This concentration was undisturbed by love affairs. I had seen too much—too early—to have the least desire to join in the pitiful scramble of my workmates. The very surroundings of shop life accentuated the desire of most shop girls to get married. Long hours of work and the living-in system deprived them of normal companionship of men in the leisure hours, and the wonder is that so many of the women continued to be good and kind, and self-respecting, without the incentive of a great cause, or of any interest outside their job . . . I had no vocation for wifehood or motherhood, but an urge to serve the union."

Margaret was chairperson of the Adult Suffrage Society. In 1906, she said in a speech, "I work for Adult Suffrage because I believe it is the quickest way to establish a real sex-equality . . . I have always said in my speeches and in conversation that these women who believe in the same terms as men Bill have a perfect right to go on working for that Bill, and I say good luck to them and may they get in! But don't let them come and tell me that they are working for my class."

Margaret was completely against the idea that only certain women should be given the vote. She believed that a limited franchise would hurt the working class. Because of these views she was unpopular with many middle-class suffragettes who though that limited franchise was an important step in their struggle.

In 1908, Margaret resigned from the Shop Assistants' Union and became secretary of the Women's Labour League. She was also active in the Women's Co-operative Guild, which was working for minimum wage legislation and improved child welfare.

In 1910, the Liberal Government asked Margaret to join their Advisory Committee on the Health Insurance Bill. She convinced the government to include maternity benefits and also influenced their decision to make the benefit the property of the mother.

On August 10, 1914, the government announced that they were releasing all suffragettes from prison. In return, the WSPU agreed to give up their militant activities to help the war effort.

In 1923, Margaret became one of the first women to enter the House of Commons. She was elected Labour MP for Northampton. In 1924, when Ramsay McDonald became Prime Minister, he appointed Margaret as parliamentary secretary to the Minister of Labour.

"Broadly speaking, I learned to recognize sin as the refusal to live up to the enlightenment we possess: to know the right order of values and deliberately to choose the lower ones: to know that, however much these values may differ with different people at different stages of spiritual growth, for one's self there must be no compromise with that which one knows to be the lower value." — Margaret Bondfield

When the 1928 Equal Franchise Act was passed, Margaret was quoted saying, "Since I have been able to vote at all I have never felt the same enthusiasm because the vote was the consequence of possessing property rather than the consequence of being a human being . . . At last we are established on that equitable footing because we are human beings and part of society as a whole."

Ramsay McDonald became Prime Minister a second time in 1929, and he appointed Margaret as his new Minister of Labour. This made Margaret the first woman to ever gain a place in the British Cabinet. However, she lost her seat in the 1931 General Election, after which she had a breakdown and several health problems.

Margaret Bondfield died at Verecroft Nursing Home on June 16, 1953.

Mary Macarthur

Mary Macarthur was born in Glasgow on August 13, 1880, to parents John Macarthur and Anne Martin. Her parents had six children, only three of whom survived, who were all girls. Mary attended the local school and decided she wanted to become a writer after editing the school magazine.

In 1895, the family opened a drapery business in Ayr, and Mary was the bookkeeper. Her father was a member of the Conservative Party and was against the trade unions, and he sent Mary to observe a meeting of the Shop Assistants' Union. Mary listened to a speech by John Turner about how poorly workers were treated by their employers and was converted to the cause of the trade unions. Mary became secretary to the Ayr branch of the Shop Assistants' Union. At a socialist meeting, she met and fell in love with Will Anderson, a member of the Independent Labour Party.

In 1902, Mary met and became friends with Margaret Bondfield, who encouraged her to attend the union's national conference and later recalled, "I had written to welcome her into the Union, but, when she came to meet me at the station, I was overcome with a sense

of a great event. Here was genius, allied to boundless enthusiasm and leadership of a high order, coming to build our little union into a more effective instrument." Mary was later elected to the union's national executive. Her political activities began to set her at odds with her father, who hated socialism. Will Anderson proposed to Mary but she wanted to have a career and moved to London in 1903 to become Secretary of the Women's Trade Union League. Mary was a member of the Independent Labour Party in London where she worked closely with two fellow Scots, Ramsay MacDonald and James Keir Hardie. In 1905, she was involved in the Exhibition of Sweated Industries and helped form the Anti-Sweating League a year later. She founded the *Women Worker*, a monthly newspaper for women trade unionists, in 1907. It later became a weekly paper and had a reach of about twenty thousand people.

Mary inspired many women to join the movement, including Dorothy Jewson and Susan Lawrence, who both became Labour Party MPs. She was active in women's suffrage, and was against the idea of limited franchise, believing it would hurt the working class. This made her unpopular with many middle-class suffragettes who saw it as an important stepping stone. Mary was also involved in the campaign for a legal minimum wage. In the summer of 1911 she organized around two thousand women in twenty strikes in Bermondsey and other parts of London.

Mary finally married Will Anderson, who had followed her to London, on September 21, 1911. Their first child died at birth in 1913, but they had a daughter two years later, named Anne Elizabeth. Anderson was elected to the House of Commons in 1914 to represent Sheffied Attercliffe, but he was defeated in 1918. Mary was also a Labour candidate in Stourbridge but was defeated in the 1918 General Election, along with many others who opposed World War I.

Mary was devastated when her husband died in the 1919 influenza epidemic. However, she continued to work with the Women's Trade

Union League and helped turn it into the Women's section of the Trade Union Congress. She developed cancer in 1920, and after two unsuccessful operations died on January 1, 1921.

Elizabeth Cady Stanton

Elizabeth Cady Stanton was born November 12, 1815 to parents Daniel Cady and Margaret Livingston in Kingstown, New York. Her father was a lawyer and made no secret of the fact that he would have preferred another son rather than a daughter. She showed an early desire to excel in intellectual pursuits. In 1832 she graduated from Emma Willard's Troy Female Seminary and was soon drawn to the abolitionist and women's movements after being influenced by her cousin Gerrit Smith, a reformer.

In 1840, Elizabeth married reformer Henry Stanton (they omitted the word "obey" from their marriage vows) and they immediately left for the World's Anti-Slavery Convention in London, where she joined other women who objected to being excluded from the assembly.

The couple went on to have seven children. Henry was a lawyer and the family eventually settled in Seneca Falls, New York.

In July 1848, Elizabeth joined with Lucretia Mott and several other women to hold the Seneca Falls Convention. The people who attended this gathering drew up a "Declaration of Sentiments" stating that women should be granted the right to vote. She met Susan B. Anthony in the early 1850s and became one of the leading voices in the women's movement. She promoted women's rights in general, such as the right to divorce, and particularly the right to vote.

During the Civil War, Elizabeth focused her efforts on abolishing slavery, but afterwards continued to fight for women's suffrage. In 1868, she worked with Susan B. Anthony on the Revolution, a militant weekly paper. The following year the two women formed the National Woman Suffrage Association. Elizabeth was the organization's first president, a position she held until 1890. At that time the NWSA merged with another group to form the National American Woman Suffrage Association, and she served as president of that organization for two years.

"We hold these truths to be self-evident: that all men and women are created equal." — Elizabeth Cady Stanton

Elizabeth traveled often to give lectures and speeches. She also worked with Susan B. Anthony on the first three volumes of the *History of Woman Suffrage*, along with Matilda Joslyn Gage, who worked with the two women on parts of the project.

Elizabeth argued that the *Bible* and organized religion played a part in oppressing women. Along with her daughter, Harriet Stanton Blatch, she published *The Woman's Bible*. The first volume was published in 1895 and the second in 1898. This publication alienated her from many in the suffrage movement.

Elizabeth died on October 26, 1902.

Matilda Joslyn Gage

Matilda Joslyn was born March 24, 1826 in Cicero, New York, to parents Hazekiah Joslyn and Helen Leslie. Her father was a doctor and an abolitionist, and the family's home was a part of the Underground Railroad.

In 1845, Matilda married Henry Hill Gage, a merchant. The couple went on to have four children and their home also became a stop on the Underground Railroad. The couple were occupied with their family and with anti-slavery activities, but Matilda was drawn to the women's suffrage movement. She was unable to attend the first Women's Rights Convention in Seneca Falls in 1848, but she went to the third convention in Syracuse in 1852. She became known as a speaker and writer on women's suffrage. During the Civil War, Matilda organized hospital supplies for Union soldiers.

Matilda was a founding member of the National Woman Suffrage Association and served in several offices of the organization. She helped organize the New York and Virginia state suffrage associations, and was an officer in the New York branch for twenty years. From 1878 to 1881 she published the official newspaper of the NWSA, the *National Citizen Ballot Box*.

In 1871, Matilda and many other women across the country attempted to vote. When Susan B. Anthony successfully voted in the 1872 presidential election and was consequently arrested, Matilda aided and supported her during her trial. In 1880, Matilda led 102 Fayetteville women to the polls when New York law allowed women to vote in the school districts where they paid their taxes.

During the 1870s, Matilda became outspoken about the brutal mistreatment of Native Americans. She became an honorary member of the Wolf Clan of the Mohawk nation

"There is a word sweeter than Mother, Home or Heaven; that word is Liberty." — Matilda Gage

and was given the name Ka-ron-ien-ha-wi, which means Sky Carrier. She was inspired by the Six Nation Iroquois Confederacy's form of government, in which "the power between the sexes was nearly equal."

Matilda worked with Stanton and Anthony on *The History of Women's Suffrage* and also wrote the pamphlets *Woman as Inventor* (1870), *Woman's Rights Catechism* (1871), and *Who Planned the Tennessee Campaign of 1862?* (1880). She was discouraged with how the suffrage movement was progressing in the 1880s and alarmed at the idea of the emergence of a Christian state, so she formed the Women's National Liberal Union in 1890, to fight the religious movement to unite church and state. In 1983, she published her book Woman, Church and State. Matilda remained a supporter of women's rights, but focused on religious issued for much of her later life.

Matilda Gage died in Chicago, Illinois on March 18, 1898.

Alice Paul

Alice Paul was born January 11, 1885 in Mount Laurel, New Jersey. She was the oldest of four children born to parents William Paul and Tacie Parry. Her father was a wealth Quaker businessman. Both parents were supporters of gender equality and education for women. Alice's mother brought her to women's suffrage meetings.

Alice attended Swathmore College, a Quaker school that was cofounded by her grandfather. She graduated in 1905 with a degree in biology. Afterwards she attended the New York School of Philanthropy (now Columbia University) and earned a Master of Arts degree in sociology in 1907. She then went to England to study social work, and after returning to the United States earned a PhD from the University of Pennsylvania in 1910.

While she was in England, Alice met American Lucy Burns and joined the women's suffrage movement there. They learned militant tactics such as picketing and hunger strikes. Once back in the United States in 1912, the two women joined the National American Woman Suffrage Association, with Alice running the Washington D.C. branch. The NAWSA focused mostly on state-by-state campaigns, while Alice preferred to lobby Congress for an amendment to the

Constitution, so she and others split from the NAWSA to form the National Woman's Party.

Alice organized pickets and parades in support of women's suffrage. Her first, and largest, was in Washington D.C. on March 3, 1913, the day before Woodrow Wilson's inauguration. Around eight thousand women marched down Pennsylvania Avenue from the Capitol to the White House while half a million spectators watched, some in support and some to harass the marchers. On March 17, Alice and other suffragists met with Wilson, who refused to amend the Constitution. Alice organized a demonstration on April 7 and founded the Congressional Union for Woman Suffrage to focus specifically on lobbying Congress.

In January of 1917, Alice and a thousand other "Silent Sentinels" started eighteen months of picketing the White House, standing at the gates with signs that read things like "Mr.

"There will never be a new world order until women are part of it." — Alice Paul

President, how long must women wait for liberty?" They were verbally and physically attacked by spectators, which got worse once the US entered World War I. The police, rather than protecting the women's free speech, arrested them on charges of obstructing traffic. Alice was sentenced to seven months in jail, where she organized a hunger strike. Doctors force fed her and threatened to send her to an asylum, but accounts in the newspapers of her treatment garnered public sympathy and support for her cause. In 1918, Wilson announced his support of women's suffrage. Two years later the Senate, House, and the required thirty-six states approved the amendment. Afterward, Alice and the National Women's Party focused on the Equal Rights Amendment, which would guarantee women constitutional protection from discrimination.

Alice continued to fight for women's rights until she had a debilitating stroke in 1974. She died on July 9, 1977.

Lucy Burns

L ucy Burns was born July 29, 1879 in Brooklyn, New York, to parents Edward and Ann Burns. She was the fourth of eight children in the Irish Catholic family. Her father was a banker and supported her education. She graduated from Vassar College in 1902. She then taught English for two years at Erasmus High School in Brooklyn, then pursued post-graduate work at Yale University. Lucy then moved to Germany and studied at the Universities of Bonn and Berlin, then Oxford.

Lucy left Oxford to join the Women's Social and Political Union, the women's suffrage organization headed by Emmeline Pankhurst. From 1909 to 1912 she was an organizer for this cause. There she met Alice Paul, a fellow American suffragist. The two women returned to the United States to work in the women's movement there. They both preferred the militant tactics that they had learned in England. They led their first march in 1913, a day before Woodrow Wilson's inauguration, with the support of the National American Woman Suffrage Association. Lucy and Alice Paul then formed the Congressional Union for Woman Suffrage, which was affiliated with the NAWSA, before breaking with that organization to form the National Woman's Party in 1916. This split had to do with the militant tactics that the two women preferred and also the fact that the NAWSA was working to secure the vote for women state-by-state, while the NWP wanted to lobby congress directly.

The NWP held marches and picketed the White House. They were arrested a number of times for crimes such as loitering or obstructing traffic. Lucy spent more time imprisoned than any other suffragist activist. The women were treated badly in prison. Lucy was handcuffed with her hands over her head, put in solitary confinement and force fed after going on a hunger strike for nineteen days.

> "I think, with never-ending gratitude, that the young women of today do not and can never know at what price their right to free speech and to speak at all in public has been earned." — Lucy Burns

Once women were given the right to vote, Lucy lived a private life in Brooklyn and was no longer politically active. She said, "I don't want to do anything more. I think we have done all this for women, and we have sacrificed everything we possessed for them, and now let them fight for it. I am not going to fight any more." Lucy and her sisters then focused on raising her orphaned niece. She died in Brooklyn on December 22, 1966.

Emmeline Pankhurst

Emmeline Goulden was born in Manchester, England on July 14, 1898 to parents Robert and Sophia Goulden. She was the eldest of ten children. Her parents were both abolitionists and supporters of women's suffrage. Her mother took her to her first suffragist meeting when she was fourteen. However, Emmeline was unhappy with the fact that her parents prioritized their sons' educations over hers.

After studying abroad in Paris, Emmeline returned to Manchester, where she met Dr. Richard Pankhurst in 1878. Richard was a lawyer and supporter of women's suffrage. Although he was twenty-four years her senior, the two married in December of 1879. Over the next ten years, Emmeline gave birth to five children: daughters Christabel, Sylvia, and Adela and sons Frank (who died young) and Harry. She remained active in politics, campaigning for her husband during his runs for Parliament (which were ultimately unsuccessful) and hosting political gatherings in their home.

In 1889, Emmeline became a supporter of the Women's Franchise League, which was against limited franchise and wanted to secure the vote for all women. Her husband supported her in these endeavors until his death in 1898. Emmeline spent the next few years coping with her grief, but still had a passion for women's rights. In 1903, she decided to create a new women-only group that focused on voting rights, the Women's Social and Political Union. Their slogan was "Deeds Not Words."

In 1905, Emmeline's daughter Christabel and fellow WSPU member Annie Kenney went to a meeting to demand to know if the Liberal party would support women's suffrage. Both women were arrested in a confrontation with police. The attention that their arrests garnered encouraged the WSPU to use more militant tactics than other suffrage groups at the time. Emmeline would encourage

"We were called militant, and we were quite willing to accept the name. We were determined to press this question of the enfranchisement of women to the point where we were no longer to be ignored by the politicians."
— Emmeline Pankhurst

the WSPU to rein in their demonstrations when it seemed like a bill on women's suffrage might move forward, but protests would escalate when the group was disappointed—like in 1910 and 1911, when Conciliation Bills failed to advance.

In 1912, Emmeline was sentenced to nine months in jail for throwing a rock at the prime minister's home. She went on a hunger strike, and rather than being force fed like many of her peers, was soon released. In order to end hunger strikes, the Prisoners' Temporary Discharge for Ill Health was enacted, which stated that prisoners who were released for health reasons could be rearrested once they had recovered. It became known as the "Cat and Mouse Act." By 1913, their tactics included window-breaking, vandalism, and arson. That same year, an incendiary device went off in an unoccupied house being built for the chancellor of the exchequer, David Lloyd George. Emmeline received a sentence of three years of penal servitude for inciting the crime. She was released after going on another hunger strike, but because of the Cat and Mouse Act she was rearrested and released several times. During one interval out of prison, Emmeline went to the United States for a fundraising and lecturing tour.

During World War I, Emmeline called for an end to militancy and demonstrations. All WSPU prisoners were released and she encouraged women to join in the war effort and fill factory jobs. Because of women's contributions to the war effort, the government granted them limited voting rights in 1918—for women who met a property requirement and were thirty years of age or older (the voting age for men was twenty-one). In 1919, another bill gave women the right to be elected to Parliament.

All of Emmeline's daughters had been members of the WSPU at some point, but she was only able to celebrate the achievement of limited franchise with one of her daughters, Christabel, her favorite. Her daughter Sylvia was a pacifist and disagreed with her mother's attitude toward the war, and Adela had moved to Australia.

Emmeline still wanted unlimited women's suffrage, but she changed focus after the war. She was worried about the rise of Bolshevism and became a member of the Conservative Party. She ran for a seat in Parliament, but her campaign was interrupted by bad health, which was exacerbated by Sylvia giving birth to an illegitimate child. She died in London on June 14, 1928. Very soon after, on July 2, 1928, Parliament gave all women the right to vote.

Nina Otero

Adalina (Nina) Otero was born in 1881 in La Constancia, New Mexico, close to Las Lunas. She was the second child of Manuel B. Otero and Eloisa Luna Otero, who both had family history in New Mexico, her mother's family dating back to early pioneers and her father's family dating back to Spanish pioneers of the eighteenth century. They were a wealthy and influential family and owned large pieces of land.

When Nina was less than two years old, her father was killed over a land dispute at the age of twenty-three. Her mother was pregnant with her third child at the time. Their extended family looked after them, and in 1886, Eloisa married Alfred Maurice Bergere, an Englishman who had immigrated to the U.S. at the age of sixteen. The couple went on to have nine children, and so the household grew to four boys and eight girls.

Nina studied at St. Vincent Academy in Albuquerque until she was eleven, then was sent to Maryville College of the Sacred Heart in St. Louis, Missouri. She returned home from school at the age of thirteen and shared what she had learned with her younger brothers and sisters. She took pride in her family's land and working on a rancho, and spent much of her time on horseback. She later wrote a book about working on ranches called *Old Spain in Our Southwest*.

Bibliography

Living My Life by Emma Goldman

Cool Women by Dawn Chipman, Mari Florence, Naomi Wax
Women's Experience in America: A Historical Anthology edited by
Esther Katz and Anita Rapone

theanarchistlibrary.org

encyclopedia.com

thefamouspeople.com

biography.com

smithsonianmag.com

womenshistory.org

sojournertruth.org

history.com

pioneeringwomen.bwaf.org

broughttolife.sciencemuseum.org.uk

bbc.co.uk

spartacus-educational.com

womenshistory.org

Colleen Glen is from Block Island, a small island off the coast of Rhode Island. She spent several years traveling the country before settling in New York City and becoming involved with the feminist community there.